WHAT URGE WILL SAVE US

Alina Pleskova

Spooky Girlfriend Press
2017

What Urge Will Save Us
All poems copyright © 2017 by Alina Pleskova.

Art: Ashley Robin Franklin
Design: Nate Logan

Spooky Girlfriend Press publishes chapbooks occasionally.
Sometimes they're, excuse me, pretty fucking great.

www.spookygirlfriendpress.tumblr.com

I used to ask that you be happy, but now I want you unbeholden to anyone in this far from credible cosmos.

— Alice Notley, "Cuticle"

WHAT URGE WILL SAVE US NOW THAT SEX WON'T?

— Jenny Holzer, Survival Series

CONTENTS

Q TRAIN POEM

My favorite New York
pastime is sobbing

You do it on the way
like everything else

Like everything else,
nobody double-takes

Small relief to be translucent
without repercussion

Slacken responsibility
for The State of Things

Headphones so I can't say
what it sounds like

Styrofoam container
between knees

29 soon & as this year,
the year before, going back

to when I thought it would
begin, but no—

I'll not have learned
to still myself

Almost never take home
strangers now

In place of their predictable
& idyllic demands, I wonder

how many more Real Loves
I'll cycle through

Or as Tom Waits put it, *who you
wanna go in the woods with*

Even when I get off, the shudder
feels hostile

Can't make the erotic subtle
or write one graceful poem

Inner monologue dubbed
by fortune cookies:

*It may be time to explore new ways
of regaining balance*

Aberrant December lets us feel okay
longer, though not without guilt

Today felt too fragile for strategizing
&/or engagement &/or collaboration

&/or proving my value to *our* stakeholders
so called out, wore leggings that made

my ass look, excuse me, pretty fucking great
& paid off some but not all my bills

& basked in the unnatural warmth
of our dying planet

It felt, excuse me,
pretty fucking great

But I've just circled back
to mama's years-old advice—

You can't sit on two chairs
comfortably at once

So let's cry about it
even though this is no time

for consolidating the tattered
concept of monogamy

Glittery teardrop settled
atop my blinchiki

Lonesome traveler
rattling with the Q

As it shoots toward
skyline, river-glint,

The deepspace
of what else

MAGPIE

Alone now
but like, radically

Turns out no such creature steals
shiny objects for a nest

I spent a while verifying this;
folklore so rarely runs parallel

to reality & the afternoon
plainly wasted already

No afterglow & no one left
on the to-do list

Same reflexive satisfaction
as after a bland meal

◇ ◇ ◇

What wants are left?
said new someone

& I sped through every welt,
every well-worn route to sunrise,

every kink indulged until
fringe turned its own vanilla,

every throat-pulse caught & held
throbbing, some name escaped as hiss

mine accented as a languid stretch:

Ahhhh

leeena on a bus with summer cunt
post-fuck stench summoning

every stillness where the shudder
should've been &

every cheery shower whistle
after

◊ ◊ ◊

Gala says of her girlfriend,

I summoned her,
now I deal with her

Devotion like the best curse
you can hope to suffer

Once, we held out for months
waiting to learn who was crueler

& I wanted you to win;
call it a masochism loop

or caged bird blues or
as a favorite ex put it,

People can tolerate infinite
damage of this variety

◊ ◊ ◊

What's left to want if the door
is always left unlatched?

Hey yea still up,
come press here—

It's never enough
but at luckiest,

the white light holds
for an instant

WONDER WHEEL

Jack, I found the blistered tip
of summer

Swinging over the peninsula's edge,
a stoned русалка run ashore in

Little Odessa with pastel wig
slanted, petrified in lip gloss

Viewed from above, this place springs
a leak in my limbic system

Waiting for parents & their friends to
shop for discount furs

Upturn in adolescent perversions & the black box
glowing with bad channels just loud enough

Knees in the carpet, figuring out how
to make myself shake & shake

in a way no visitor could replicate
or even mimic

I kept a careful guest book
anyway,

*s next to those
who came closest

◇ ◇ ◇

I'm talking out my want,
Jack

& I'm trying to remember which
where I'm in now

Hang back in a mother tongue haze
shaping Cyrillic aloud

I only want to say аптека,
say русский кассеты,

say останься со мной,
but that's later

◊ ◊ ◊

We've been never since the start
& what to do with it now

I don't know if a poem could
go on forever, Jack, as you say

but Kim wrote on Twitter
What else do we ruin our lives for

& Alice Notley wrote,
I'll fuck up your life your cute life

& Masha Tupitsyn wrote, on Alice Notley,
Why shouldn't you not know what hit you?

I thought it'd be more years of
men repeating my jokes louder

instead I swallowed
something electric

what I mean is, how doomed are we
who despite our intelligence

believe in retrograde panic &
the redemptive properties

        of shoegaze
        raspberry kush
        ceiling fans

       blue moon magic
       sage
       the pull-out method

   a trap street in England called Lye Close

  it all might be real

If no feeling's final
I'll pick a point to steady myself

call it horizon or
the simulacrum

I hold fast anyway & see for how long
Jack, if you keep me talking

One day, I'll tell you what
I'm really thinking about

DON'T CALL ME, I'M PRACTICING FOR OUR THREESOME

Thoughts all sing-song like
Nobody knows where I am right now

Stroll the wrong way with dress
trailing mid-air when all the bars

let out & some bodies come so close,
we pass right through each other

Every jolt of pleasure attuned at once,
a shock to the system

The clock tower chimes an alarm for those
of us tensed & ready to walk the high-wire

from ardor to fury & back again
when we wake

13th Street starlets fan out their lashes
curbside, holler *Get it, honey*

which I take to mean:
Quit sleeping easy

& shimmy down a backstreet
to slip off all this reserve

The uncertainty itself
suddenly enough

ACE OF CUPS

In an alternate version of today,
I corner each whim with a lullaby

> *Hush—there's nothing interesting*
> *about a resistible urge*

Instead, a card left face up so
its forces leak, lap the hours

We indecisive are most receptive
to rituals, for want of what

more to do when
waiting for what's next

Boldened by last night's harvest-
bright glow, I flung sage ash

onto the stoop & said *Shitty energies*
be gone in a touch too-civil tone

Continued in today's itinerary of walking
to forget motion's the only goal

A want to not believe in goals
disconcertingly a goal itself

◇ ◇ ◇

Botch divinity yr own way: it's the
freestyle round of sentience

Pick an amulet like evil eye, opal, or
more pink pills bisected into crescents

Then tilt skyward for cloudy viscera
of a crystal ball & attempt prognosis

or else stumble on

◇ ◇ ◇

To relinquish logic is to let sense
& reflex swerve

Trip over a cobblestone loose
since always, even though I know

better & still do when sliding
uncovered into the hottest patch of sun

just to make those fading teeth-marks
gleam a red bloom
                              for sheer love of mementos

Scan ledes & the weekly horoscopes
of still-relevant loves while mine advises

spiritually adopt hedonism: a clear signal
to lose the plan altogether

& claw harder into what
I want to take along

Let the hungry ghost gorge
Try & keep it down this time

SONG OF THE MELANCHOLY SLUT

When the universe winks,
I wink back reflexively

As now, "Part-Time Lover"
on the taxi radio & my head

half out the window
grinning at bleached sky

on waterway, this life caught
in a protracted moment of buffering

Stevie's talk of illicitness
& discretion rings quaint:

an affair, in its exactitude, marks
the lover as wrong, full stop

A useless gauge if the stakes
aren't so linear, as here

In Durak, the player left holding
cards is deemed the fool

There's no option to fold
if you foresee it–

wait for defeat or play like
you don't know it's coming

I haven't decided to leave you
yet, but I can envision it today

in this pocket of bliss, my body
hazed with yr brackish stink

Last week, I tried to lose a man
at the art museum, but he kept

appearing, palm on my back,
to ask what I thought. I thought

only of a lost capacity to ignore
discord for carnality's sake

Dura, dura sang Vadim
when I lost. The table laughed

& so did I. That's how it goes:
I don't know I'm a *dura* until

the universe winks & I squint
to determine whether

it's an illusion. As if knowing
alters the outcome

SATURN RETURN

Everyone hurries a touch in the moody weather
while I reach peak Aquarius: calmer in risk's orbit,

ruthlessly down for whatever, even or especially if it stings
Good morning, universe, with yr sudden biting air—

My erotic imagination remains on sabbatical despite
many blessings in the house of novel apparatus

& the alleged libido spike tied to this astrological transit
as consolation for its relentless cataclysms

I tried to look moved when you showed me
a vibrator that doubles as an alarm clock

though most days, I wake trembling around
the edges & think, *What rot awaits?*

which cancels out both my OPTIMUM CHILL banner
& the energy-cleansing effects of a Himalayan salt lamp

my mother gave me because she suspects
I'll never produce grandchildren

This may be true, since our economic system
is structurally rigged to fuck the working class

& for this, my dirty chakras
aren't to blame

◇ ◇ ◇

Based on break room discourse, the
approaching cuffing season isn't nearly

as kinky as it sounds, & hinges on
a crude sense of urgency

Back in my reality, some friends
avoid saying *partner*

as it indicates a hierarchy
& this harshes the egalitarian vibe

I don't seem to fall into either camp:
power dynamics maintain their hobbyist appeal

while having a primary partner
sublimates me into a gentler form

To demonstrate why this is important,
I gesture now at the unstable world

◇ ◇ ◇

More than 100,000 want to go to Mars
& not return reads the headline

Well, I'll wait right here & bore a path into
the center of the earth using just my anxiety

or carry out the neoliberal conspiracy
of self-care: *Rumours* on repeat

& a man-repellant shade of lipstick
named *Dirty Money*— smudge-proof

for all those late late-capitalist nights
spent tidying this condition to let someone in

After returning from a wedding, I dart
around him for days, just in case

nesting is a communicable state

or desire molds to its closest container

When he sends a fresh batch
of dick pics, my equilibrium returns

in the stillness
of remembering

we're all just dopamine vampires
trying to skirt the mortal coil

Bleak humor suits
my Soviet blood

& everything does feel fine
when Rachel says

Do you know anybody
who is okay right now

with the question mark
deliberately left out

Reclaiming my life
meant divesting

explains an article about hoarding
As if I get to choose how long

her muted perfume clings, or apply
logic like a compress to the forehead

The difficulty of divesting isn't
in the discarding—

it's in knowing what to keep
But I recall our particulars all wrong

which is to say incandescently

which is to say I romanticize
the lack of understanding that keeps

predictability or comfort
from permeating "our thing"

Nothing's nailed down in this liminal space
of torpor & grope

Limp parts left out in case of mood lifts

Drape swell & recede

Hoarse mouth suckling a shoulder

Language held taut

& this oracular heart of mine resigned
to hit snooze again

So much for yr fixed sign
& a wobbled laugh on delay

ALIGHT

First 48 hours post-landing are
the sweet spot: part troposphere,

brain a bundle of unguarded nerves,
generous to every rush of perception

Swayed by how locals say *That's alright*,
hand wave putting kindness back into the air

instead of *You're welcome*, as in
a transfer of something owed

After two carafes of wine, burrow back
into someone else's word-hovel

All hangover, all hummingbird-hearted,
a bundle of sensitivities

Ariana Reines says
It's dangerous to have feelings when you don't have any money

But corporate's got this
so I'm selling out

so I'm crying in the battery-powered
candlelight of this overpriced brasserie

◇ ◇ ◇

One day per time zone is the accepted
recovery rate for jet lag

Maybe this applies to other bodily phenomena
like vulnerability, wherever that gets made

Hacking body with light could speed jet lag recovery
explains the Internet

I'm a feelings hack;
it wasn't always this way

I used to trust them, whatever
they were in the moment, to lead

◇ ◇ ◇

To fall in love with anyone
all you need to do is answer

36 questions, says the *Times*
hey, I was wondering—

Do you have a secret
hunch about how you will die?

◇ ◇ ◇

It took an acid trip to dredge
my first love epiphany to surface

Allie said, *What are you afraid of?*
while I shook in the pitch-dark woods

Being so certain

◇ ◇ ◇

Brits are indiscriminate with terms of endearment
despite their low thresholds for sentimentality

darling, dearie,
love, love, love

the bus driver,
the deli cashier,
the receptionist

I mean yea, it's only
a word

but when I think of yr face,
the word becomes mist

When I tell myself to think on that, the thought ricochets
so I shut the light off

◇ ◇ ◇

Today, the giant bruise on the back of my arm
tinges brown-blue

I've stopped romanticizing bruises as mood indicators
since they all heal basically the same

This is surely a sign of maturity

Hang my one decent blazer
to unwrinkle while I shower

Think of baking out hotel bathrooms with the one I left
& our willful roach burns

Somewhere a cloud swelling from
his drawn-out messages

I would've done it just the same without them
is what I'd say if I ever wanted it again

◇ ◇ ◇

Swish past cows, wildflower fields,
towns with fairytale names

Businessman's intermittent throat clearing
even pleasant

Futile spy with black trench, flip notebook
full of obvious things:

longing, Appleford, yellow flowers,
distance as a safety catch

Want to keep riding this train into oblivion
head suddenly absent of the usual static

Intrusions like existential dread or blanket panic or deadlines
do exist, are presently unknown

Warmed in my oversize scarf & thinking of
the Lewis Warsh poem I read to yr voicemail

because it had the lines

Denying something, I sometimes
think, is the same as admitting
it. I admit you into my thoughts
without even trying.

& I do, & now it's time
to disembark

◊ ◊ ◊

Thought I'd chain smoke around the clock here
but am never relaxed enough,

upright in the open office, watching trees whip around
waiting for the poem to stop before I'm found out

or wedged between two chemists
on the train, talking molecules

while I glare into the book Emma lent me
People who want their love easy don't really want love

Slump into the seat, tune back
to the chemists & their compounds

◇ ◇ ◇

Made it this far
without mentioning the rain

Here it is;
it's perfect

Relentless as movies & that
Magnetic Fields song have us believe

I carry an umbrella & never use it,
head wrapped like a babushka instead

Another way, in my ever-expanding list of ways
to feel less American

Which is to say, elegant in the face of
my boorishness

At least my reflection
looks Russian, I think,

then call my mother & see how long I can
go without English interludes

But I forget the word for restless,
though she's been saying it

my whole life long

NOW THAT I AM IN REYKJAVIK AND CAN THINK

After the ring road followed wide & serpentine for hours,
headlong run through knee-level mud, now agape in a lava field

where Joe & Ryan pick crowberries for jam, chattering in
the secret dialect lovers take on after enough years together,

I think of you

& *The Ethical Slut*, 2nd edition, Chapter 7: "Abundance",
wherein the authors lay out their argument against

a starvation economy approach to love, how it's not this
finite resource, so shake off yr cultural programming

& the desire to possess— instead, get better at scheduling,
an art I can't execute with any finesse & that's partly why

I'm here without you or any of the others, though one of
yr curls held fast all this way, until it lifted off

& landed in the cushioned moss, which grows so slowly
with an idea of order I totally admire but cannot fathom.

◇ ◇ ◇

Here as home as anywhere, I'm a Laelaps in runny nylons
roaming from mouth to mouth, secrets left intact

in the babble before I return to mortal with wholesome hemline,
then the harbor solo to gape dumb at the midnight sunset

& wonder if one can bore into another with such precision
that the hunger is perfect & all you sense, even in summer,

these long stretches with no darkness as a comfort to settle you,
so every big idea dilutes into a buoyant postcard signed *Yours*

as in sending love from this smoky cove flush
with episodic arguments in favor of constant motion,

each gorgeous detail the only one of its kind
& the mind's dazed shutter relentless to capture

this sublimity, this proof we should be tender,
given our undoing breezes in just the same

◇ ◇ ◇

As muscle memory is made stubborn,
so it can reprogram: like the trick where

I pinch longing mid-shudder, save it for another
time, get the shower good & scalding,

head out divine & untethered
into the endless day

Acknowledgments

Thank you to the editors of *Queen Mob's Tea House, Public Pool, Mistress, Vagabond City Lit, Sea Foam Mag,* and *littletell,* in which many of these poems or versions of these poems first appeared.

Love & so much gratitude to Andrew Clark, Thomson Guster, Brandon Holmquest, Ryan Eckes, Patrick Blagrave, Sebastian Castillo, Emma Sanders, Mel Bentley, & Rachel Milligan for yr generosity & insight; to Jackee Sadicario, for holding up the other end of the dreamiest creative partnership I've ever had; to мои русские ведьмы, Gala Mukolomova & Sonya Vatomsky, for showing me what's possible; to Jenn McCreary & Pattie McCarthy, who are everything I hope to become; to Mike Messina, for going into the woods & back.

Made in the USA
Middletown, DE
12 April 2017